# THE ART OF SAFETY

# THE ART OF SAFETY

A Workbook to Help You Transform the Words From
Frontline Incident Prevention - The Hurdle Into Action

## DAVID McPEAK

UBM
UTILITY BUSINESS MEDIA, INC.
Communication and Education That Matter

Utility Business Media from Crystal Lake, IL

The Art of Safety- A Workbook to Help You Transform the Words From Frontline Incident Prevention
- The Hurdle Into Action

Published by UBM
Utility Business Media, Inc.

ISBN (paperback): 9781662930812

# Table of Contents

# Introduction

It's difficult to jump over a hurdle standing still. This workbook will help you generate run-ups that optimize culture, people and systems that will energize and sustain exceptional safety. Upon completion, you should understand how to:

- Use the run-up of **C5 Safety Leadership** to create culture and develop relationships so you can get over the hurdle of *Lack of Leadership*
- **Lead People, Not Robots** rather than *Discounting Human Factors* by leading and managing people how they are and not how you wish they were
- Start **Protecting the Worker** with CAVE culture and stop *Pleasing the System* by settling for compliance, documentation and results alone
- Be a STAR, protect yourself, stay safe and be well by understanding the safety paradox and replacing *Overreliance on "You"* with **Self-Reliance**
- Do not use a chair as a ladder or become a human voltage detector by avoiding *Risk Tolerance* and **Unnormalizing Deviation**
- Never let the other team shoot but have a goalie just in case by inverting the *Upside Down Hierarchy* and never needing your PPE with **A New Hierarchy**

## Using this Workbook

This workbook is designed for individual study, group studies, and leadership development workshops. It corresponds to the *Frontline Incident Prevention – The Hurdle* book and iPi's *The Art of Safety* e-learning course. Ideally, you will read the relevant chapter and use this workbook to develop your personal action plan while watching applicable videos and completing related exercises inside the e-learning course. While it will maximize your learning, you do not have to enroll in the e-learning course. You will need a copy of the book to use with this workbook.

If you are using this workbook to facilitate group studies or workshops, each person will need a copy of the book and this workbook and at least one person from the group should enroll in the e-learning course so your group can watch the videos together. The most effective way is for each person to go through this workbook on their own prior to group discussions so everyone can contribute and add insights from the group to their personal notes.

Before your groups meets, establish a facilitator for the discussion. It is recommended to rotate the facilitator of each session. This person does not need to have all the answers. They will be responsible for establishing ground rules, guiding discussions, showing relevant videos, and keeping the group focused. At a minimum, your group should discuss the *Questions for Individual Reflection / Group Discussion* at the end of each section and create action items from those conversations.

You know yourself and your TEAM better than anyone. While these guidelines will optimize your learning and understanding, use whatever combination of the book, e-learning course, and this workbook in whatever way works best for you. Nail the run-ups and soar over the hurdles.

# Lack of Leadership / C5 Safety Leadership

## Incomplete Definitions

Define each of the following terms in your own words.

Leadership

Safety Leadership

Employee Involvement

## Limited Reporting

Plot the number of reports (good catches, inconsequential errors, near hits, near misses) you have received over the last 12 years (or whatever time period you have data for) and see how similar it looks to the typical reporting bell curve.

Your Reporting Graph                          Typical Reporting Bell Curve

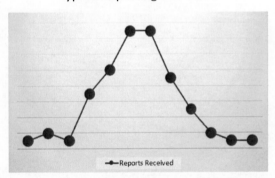

## Fear

**FEAR** stands for _____ _____ _____ _____

In the space below, keep a tally for a week of how often you tell people what to do in an autocratic way compared to how often you encourage desired behaviors.

Tell people what to do                         Encourage and explain why

Define each of the 5 "C" words in your own words and then list SMART (Specific, Measurable, Achievable, Relevant, Timely) actions you can take to grow each. Remember growing one will grow the other four and increase both your influence and authority. Focus on influence.

C

_____

C

_____

C

_____

C

_____

C

_____

## Questions for Individual Reflection / Group Discussion

1. Describe your leadership training program for current and future frontline leaders and brainstorm ideas on how it can be improved.  Better yet, ask your frontline leaders this same question.

2. Where do Us Versus Them mentalities exist and what can you do to eliminate them and encourage TEAMwork?

3. Are you satisfied with the quantity and quality of reporting you get? If not, what can you do to encourage reporting?  This may be a good time to discuss James Reason's characteristics of a successful culture.

4. In what situations are you using fear as a tactic or letting fear drive your behavior (action and inaction)? How can C5 Safety Leadership help you overcome fear?

5. What is the difference between liking and caring?  Why is it important for safety leaders to focus on caring over liking?

6. How can you gain influence rather than relying on authority?

7. What are your key takeaways from this section?

# Discounting Human Factors / Lead People, Not Robots

## Thinking of People as Robots

What do robots do and what will they not do?  How are robots different than people?

## Anatomy of an Event

Label each gray box with one of the terms on the right and then define each term in your own words.

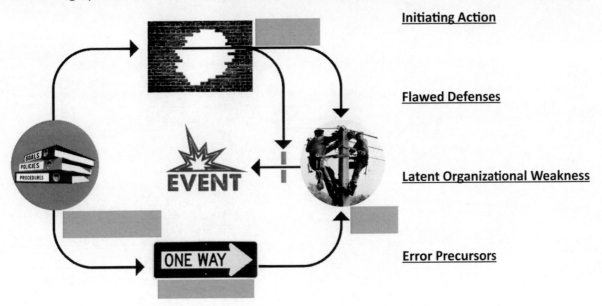

**Initiating Action**

**Flawed Defenses**

**Latent Organizational Weakness**

**Error Precursors**

## TWIN Model of Error Precursors

### TASK DEMANDS

- Time Pressure (in a hurry)
- High workload (memory requirements)
- Simultaneous, multiple tasks
- Repetitive actions, monotonous
- Irrecoverable acts
- Interpretation requirements
- Unclear goals, roles & responsibilities
- Lack of or unclear standards

### INDIVIDUAL CAPABILITIES

- Unfamiliarity with the task/First time
- Lack of knowledge (mental model)
- New technique not used before
- Imprecise communications habits
- Lack of proficiency/Inexperience
- Indistinct problem-solving skills
- Can do or Unsafe attitude for critical task
- Illness/fatigue

### WORK ENVIRONMENT

- Distractions/Interruptions
- Changes/Departures from the routine
- Confusing displays or controls
- Workarounds/OOS instruments
- Hidden system / equipment response
- Unexpected equipment conditions
- Lack of alternative indication
- Personality conflicts

### HUMAN NATURE

- Stress (limits attention)
- Habit patterns
- Assumptions (inaccurate mental picture)
- Complacency/Overconfidence
- Mindset ("tuned" to see)
- Inaccurate risk perception
- Mental shortcuts (biases)
- Limited short term memory

Source: DOE Human Performance Improvement Handbook Volume One

| | |
|---|---|
| *Error Precursor* | Anything that negatively impacts behavior and decision making; a trigger for action |
| *Questions to ask yourself and your team* | Which from Task Demands is the most common and what can we do about it? <br><br> Which from Work Environment is the most common and what can we do about it? <br><br> Which from Individual Capabilities is the most common and what can we do about it? <br><br> Which from Human Nature is the most common and what can we do about it? |
| *For each response above ask* | How could _____ negatively impact behavior and decision making? <br><br> How can we eliminate or reduce _____ \_? <br><br> How do I create _____ on my team? |

## Questions for Individual Reflection / Group Discussion

1. Things are managed and people are led. Given that, what are the ramifications of thinking about people like robots?

2. Do you tend to assign blame or seek to learn and prevent after incidents? How can you move away from the blame cycle? This may be a good time to discuss A B C D E.

3. What assumptions are you making about common sense, especially in the areas of training, evaluation, incident analysis, and observations?

4. Have you provided training on decision making tools to your frontline leaders and workers?

5. What are your key takeaways from this section?

# Pleasing the System / Protecting the Worker

## Pleasing the System Assessment

| | Never | Sometimes | Often |
|---|:---:|:---:|:---:|
| 1. Observers are required to find something wrong during jobsite observations. | 3 | 2 | 1 |
| 2. Pre-job briefings are evaluated based on the form. | 3 | 2 | 1 |
| 3. I receive/give fours on evaluations because no one here gets a five and there are surprises during evaluations. | 3 | 2 | 1 |
| 4. Our safety program incentivizes zero recordable injuries. | 3 | 2 | 1 |
| 5. Blame is assigned after incident investigations. | 3 | 2 | 1 |

**Total Score – add the number you circled from each row.**

**10 is average. 11 or above is good.** _____

## Testing the System Assessment

| | Often | Sometimes | Never |
|---|:---:|:---:|:---:|
| 1. I tell my supervisor when I feel uncomfortable doing a job or unqualified/unprepared for a task I have been assigned. | 3 | 2 | 1 |
| 2. I report good catches, inconsequential errors, near hits, and near misses. | 3 | 2 | 1 |
| 3. I correct my peers and more experienced workers as needed. | 3 | 2 | 1 |
| 4. I request additional resources (equipment, tools, people) if they are needed to complete a job safely and/or on time. | 3 | 2 | 1 |
| 5. I exercise my stop work authority during work execution. | 3 | 2 | 1 |
| 6. I ask observers, managers, peers, and supervisors for feedback, especially when it isn't offered. | 3 | 2 | 1 |
| 7. I ask questions during job briefings and training sessions. | 3 | 2 | 1 |
| 8. I point out flaws in procedures and work methods. | 3 | 2 | 1 |
| 9. I make suggestions about how things can be improved, offer new ideas, and propose solutions to challenges. | 3 | 2 | 1 |
| 10. I continue working as usual when someone is observing my performance. | 3 | 2 | 1 |

**Total Score – add the number you circled from each row.**

**20 is average.  21 or above is good.** _____

1. Complete the Pleasing the System assessment and distribute it throughout your workforce for anonymous completion. Tally and discuss the results. For anything marked 1, talk about how it can be improved.

2. Complete the Testing the System assessment and distribute it throughout your workforce for anonymous completion. Tally and discuss the results. For anything marked 1, talk about how it can be improved.

3. How can you encourage CAVE culture? Discuss how the statement *and in terms of motivation, we won't be satisfied until what we value is fulfilled* relates to the safety culture of your organization.

4. Correlate the Overview Effect to your earlier discussion from C5 Safety Leadership about Us Versus Them mentalities and TEAMwork. Discuss what it means to treat people equally while acknowledging they are never the same.

5. What are your key takeaways from this section?

# Overreliance on "You" / Self-Reliance

## The Safety Paradox

Who and what do you rely on to keep you safe.  What do you rely on these people and things to do?

Explain the meaning and intent of these two statements:

_I should work in a way that "you" is never needed._

_PPE. Always use it and never need it._

_"I am my brother's and sister's keeper."_  _"I am responsible for my own safety."_  Explain how those two statements create the safety paradox along with how and why they are not mutually exclusive.

What are your dual roles in safety?

1.

2.

## Tools

Define each of these tools in your own words and strategize how you will use them moving forward. Volume Two of the DOE HPI Handbook is a great reference for these tools.

Validate Assumptions.

Replace assumptions with F_____, A_____, C_____, T_____, S_____

While you are thinking about assumptions, the next time you see someone lifting a load (manually or with equipment), ask them how much the load weighs. It may surprise you how often they don't know and are making assumptions about physical ability and load capacity.

Self-Checking with S_____, T_____, A_____, R_____.

Questioning Attitude

Procedure Use and Adherence

Verification Practices

Define critical tasks you and your TEAM perform and how you can use each of these tools to reduce error and manage controls during those tasks.

## Questions for Individual Reflection / Group Discussion

1. Discuss how advances in protective equipment and technology present challenges to safety and what you can to encourage proper work methods.

2. Look up ANSI Z10 requirements and OSHA guidance on safety and health management systems and use them as a benchmark for your safety programs. If you identify any gaps, brainstorm and implement suggestions.

3. Is it possible to achieve error free performance for specific time periods during specific task executions? What combination of tools can you use to make sure this happens during critical tasks?

4. Are there areas you, your team, and your organization are settling for compliance? This is a good opportunity to review how job briefings are conducted and evaluated.

5. What are your key takeaways from this section?

# Risk Tolerance / Unnormalizing Deviation

Read the list of bad idea precursors or trigger statements in Hold My Beer and Watch This. Document times you use or hear them on your jobsite for a week in the space below. Train yourself and your TEAM on what is considered acceptable logic using self-checking and validating assumptions tools.

Compare how work is designed versus how work is performed, especially for critical tasks. Identify areas where NOD is occurring and work with your TEAM on procedure use and adherence.

| My (Our) Deviation | Why | Outcome | Action Item (Chage Needed) | Outcomes |
|---|---|---|---|---|
|  |  |  |  |  |
|  |  |  |  |  |
|  |  |  |  |  |
|  |  |  |  |  |

## Work Planning Tools

What are the two work planning myths that need to be dispelled and how can you debunk those myths?

1.

2.

Work with your team to incorporate two-minute drills and post-job briefings into your job briefings.

| Pre-Job Briefing | Two-Minute Drill | Post-Job Briefing |
|---|---|---|
|  |  |  |

1. Reread the Effective Job Briefings section. How will job briefings be improved and evaluated in the future (hint – your discussion should not focus on the form or documentation)?

2. Discuss how minor changes, short delays, significant changes, and extended delays will be defined and provide specific examples of each.

   Minor Changes

   Significant Changes

   Short Delays

   Extended Delays

3. What are your key takeaways from this section?

# Upside Down Hierarchy / A New Hierarchy

## Three Simple Steps

Pick a task your TEAM performs frequently and use Three Simple Steps to develop a work method for that task. Keep an open mind by eliminating risk tolerance during step one and availability and confirmation biases during steps two and three. Use this example of how to prevent backing collisions as a model.

1. Hazard and Risk Assessment
   a. Use the Risk Assessment Matrix to assess risk. For backing, I rank the probability as Likely and the severity as Critical resulting in a High risk.
   b. Use the Energy Wheel to define the type and amount of energy. For backing, it's Motion at one to ten miles per hour.
   c. Use the Intersect to understand where energy can cause harm. For backing, I am protected in my vehicle but I can cause harm to people and property so I'll focus on the task and environment.
2. Safety by Design
   a. Turn it off by eliminating the hazard or source of energy. In this case, don't back up.
   b. Turn if down by reducing the energy as much as possible. In this case, slow down while backing.
   c. Turn away means reducing exposure. In this case, reduce how far and how often I back up.
3. Defense in Depth
   a. Establish administrative controls such as get out and look or call my supervisor before backing.
   b. Establish warning devices such as back up cameras and spotters.
   c. Establish PPE for the task such as traffic vests for everyone in the area or rubber bumpers around my vehicle.

The result of your work will look something like this. Notice I included thoughts such as disabling the reverse gear and putting rubber bumpers around my vehicle that may not be plausible or practical. It is really important to be as creative and open-minded as possible during the planning stage. Put everything on the table and then decide on your work method. You can then apply that work method to specific task executions and jobs during pre-job briefings and two-minute drills.

My Backing Example       Your Task: _____

| My Backing Example | | Your Task: | |
|---|---|---|---|
| Elimination | Approved stops, cushioning, disable reverse gear, pull-thru parking, route planning | Elimination | |
| Substitution and Reduction | Back at slower speed, bigger parking lots, smaller vehicle size | Substitution and Reduction | |
| Engineering Controls and Safety Devices | Airbag, collision avoidance system | Engineering Controls and Safety Devices | |
| Administrative Controls | 360 walkaround, call supervisor before backing, GOAL, job briefings, training | Administrative Controls | |
| Warning Devices | Back-up alarms, cameras, cones, mirrors, spotters | Warning Devices | |
| PPE | Rubber bumpers, traffic vests | PPE | |

Repeat this process for frequent tasks until you have a library of JHAs and standardized work methods.

1. Do you have a fully developed JHA library for use as reference during work planning?  If not, make a plan to work with your frontline workforce to develop them.

2. How often are you settling for PPE?  What can you do to encourage frontline workers to be above the line on the HOC?

3. What opportunities are there to reduce risk?

4. What are your key takeaways from this section?

# Creating Your Run-Ups

The Creating Your Run-Ups chapter of the book proposes 120 action items you can take to achieve exceptional safety. Pick your top two from each category and develop a personalized plan to implement.

## Lack of Leadership / C5 Safety Leadership

1.

2.

## Discounting Human Factors / Lead People, Not Robots

1.

2.

## Pleasing the System / Protecting the Worker

1.

2.

## Overreliance on "You" / Self-Reliance

1.

2.

## Risk Tolerance / Unnormalizing Deviation

1.

2.

## Upside Down Hierarchy / A New Hierarchy

1.

2.

*Nail the run-ups and soar over the hurdles.*

# Notes

Made in United States
North Haven, CT
14 June 2023

37721249R00017

UBM

UTILITY BUSINESS
MEDIA, INC.

ISBN 9781662930812

90

9 781662 930812

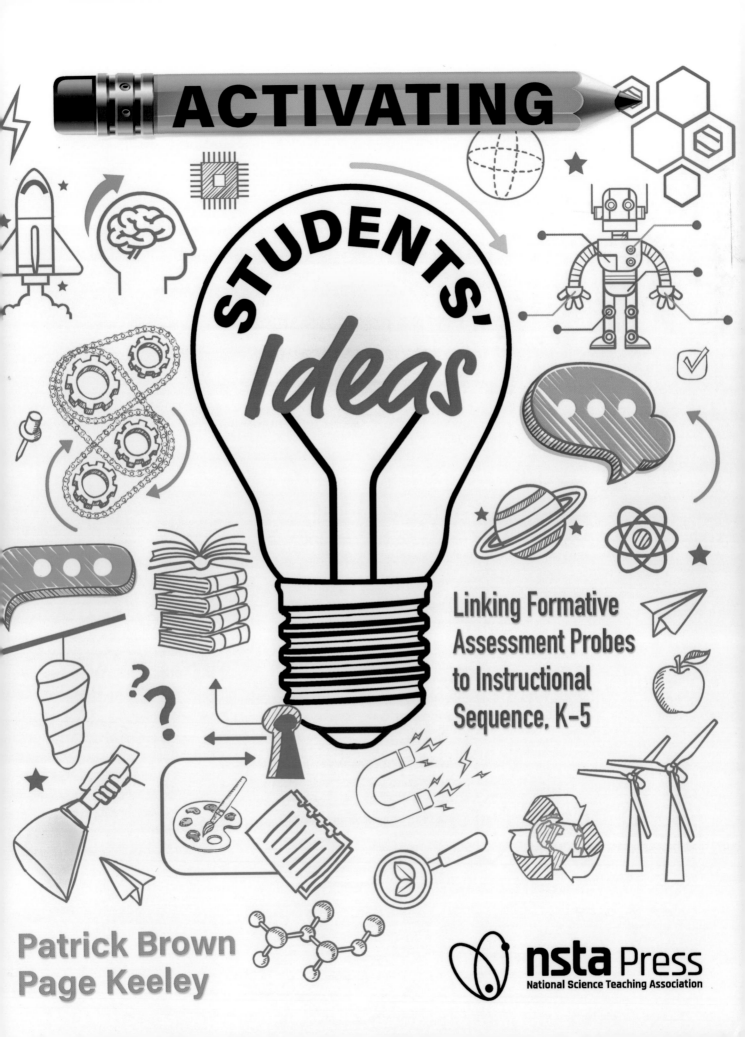

# ACTIVATING

# STUDENTS' *Ideas*

Linking Formative
Assessment Probes
to Instructional
Sequence, K–5

**Patrick Brown**
**Page Keeley**

## nsta Press
National Science Teaching Association